Photos:
Frank Gardner ("Golf World")

ISBN 0-905703-00-6

© Beaverbrook Newspapers Ltd 1975
© Chancerel Publishers Ltd 1977
for the english edition

Printed in Italy

action

BOOKS

GOLF
100 ways to improve your game

TENNIS
Basic Techniques and Tactics

PHOTOGRAPHY
Using a 35 mm camera

YOGA
The happy way to live

JUDO
The practical way

MOTORCYCLES
Maintain your own machine

SWIMMING
Learning, training, competing

GARDENING
Fruit, flowers and vegetables

MOTORCARS
Maintenance and minor repairs

FIRST AID
And emergency care

GUNCRAFT
The techniques of shooting

HOME MOVIES
Make and project your own films

GOLF

100 ways to improve your game

Peter Townsend

Script: Iain Reid

Drawings by Richard Hughes

Chancerel | BARRIE & JENKINS
COMMUNICA-EUROPA

*P*eter Townsend is a brilliant player. He is also a golfer, who has had to fight to achieve his full potential. That's what makes him especially well qualified as a golf teacher. He knows the shot for every occasion. He knows just how to play that shot. And he also appreciates the difficulties involved—especially for the average player.

Townsend was a golfing prodigy. Born in 1946, in Cambridge, he turned professional at the age of 20, after one of the most brilliant amateur careers of recent times.

His success as a professional was almost immediate. His first major win was the 1967 Dutch Open Championship. The following season he won three tournaments and topped the British Order of Merit—with £10,000 to his credit.

In 1969 he was selected for the Ryder Cup Team and played a major part in the historic tied match against the United States at Royal Birkdale.

During 1970 Townsend had a frustrating spell on the American circuit. He returned to Britain and, by sheer hard work and determination, he rebuilt one of the finest natural swings in modern golf into a consistent and winning method. He learned how to temper his natural attacking approach to golf with the right degree of caution. It is these lessons —self-taught and pursued with a single-minded dedication— that make Peter Townsend an outstanding golf teacher.

By 1971 he had once again achieved selection for the Ryder Cup side and was back in winning form. And he is still winning. In 1976 he won the ICL (South Africa) Open.

Peter Townsend is married with one child. He is attached to the famous Portmarnock Club in Co. Dublin, Eire.

Contents

Good timing is the essence of a sound swing.
And a sound swing is the cornerstone of good golf.

In showing how you can build a reliable and enduring method,
Peter Townsend explains the importance of the grip, the stance,
the takeaway and the follow - through, as well as demonstrating
the many adjustments he has made in order to perfect his method.

Of particular importance to the beginner
is the distinction between " swinging " and " hitting ".
It is the mistaken belief of many a novice, says Townsend,
that brute strength produces greater distance.

It doesn't – but timing does,
and this chapter helps you attain that elusive quality.

The swing

Good golf begins with a good grip

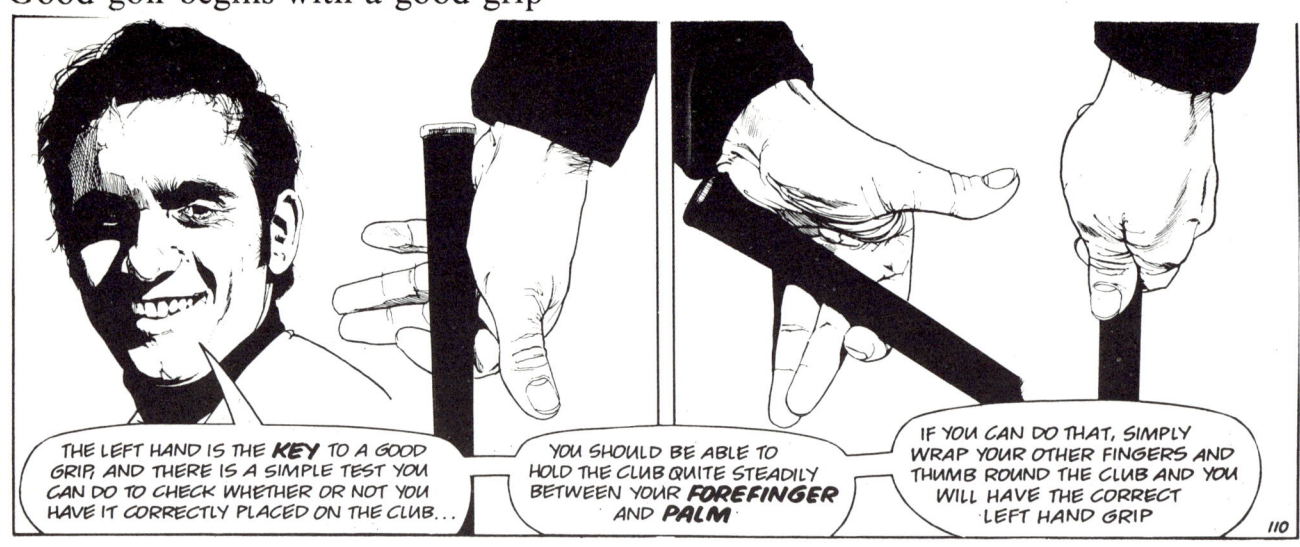

How to prevent overswinging

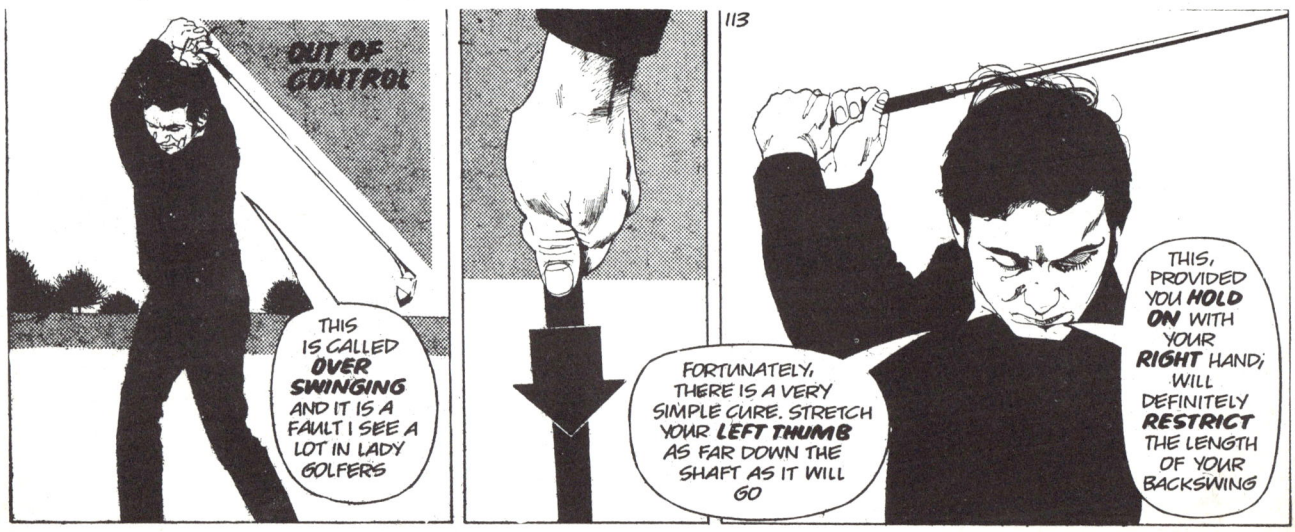

Be relaxed at address

Avoid tilting the hips

Check your left foot position

Dipping can be fatal

THIS PRODUCES *"FAT"* SHOTS AND *"THIN"* SHOTS. THE BLADE EITHER STRIKES THE *TURF* UNDER THE BALL OR CONTACTS THE *TOP* OF THE BALL !

A GOOD REMEDY IS TO IMAGINE THERE IS A *SPIKE* TOUCHING YOUR CHIN

IF YOU DIP DOWN, YOU ARE GOING TO HAVE A *NASTY ACCIDENT !*

Positioning the left shoulder

TRY TO BE IN THIS POSITION...

NOT *THIS !*

IN ORDER TO ACHIEVE THE CORRECT HITTING POSITION YOU MUST HOLD YOUR *LEFT SHOULDER HIGH* AT ADDRESS !

THIS MAKES YOU WORK *UNDER* THE BALL AND, IF YOU WORK UNDER THE BALL, YOU *CANNOT MOVE FORWARD !*

65

13

The right foot as an anchor

The club should point straight

Forget the hands

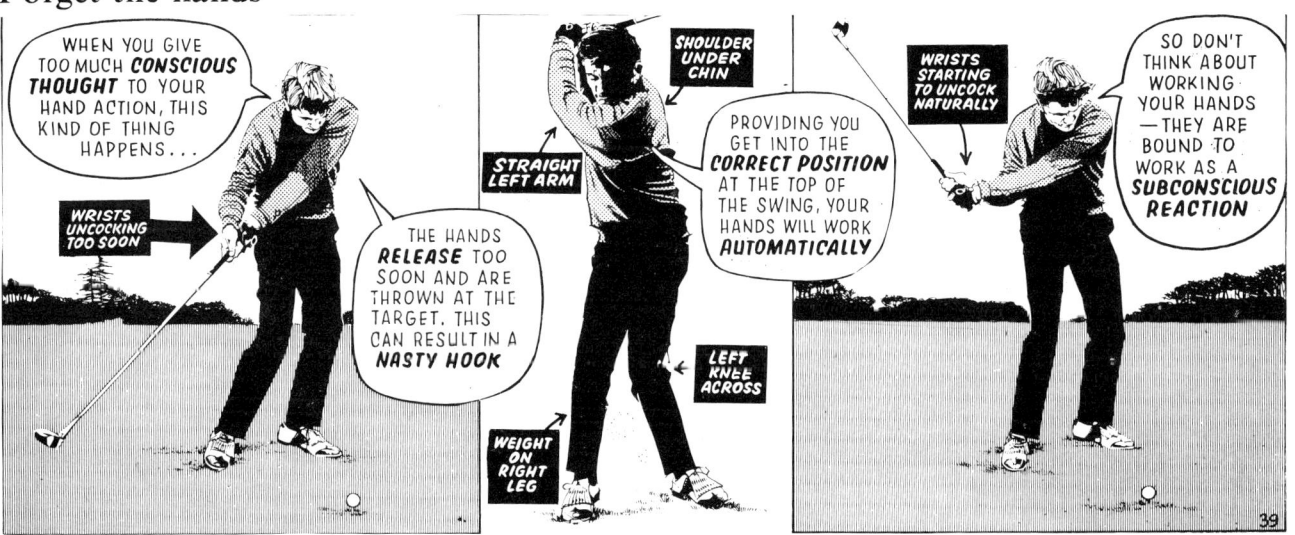

Many argue about arm positions

Your right elbow may fly out

When the swing becomes flat

FLAT

THIS IS BECAUSE, IN WIND, YOU ARE ALWAYS TRYING TO **KEEP THE BALL DOWN**. THE MORE **UPRIGHT** THE SWING THE **HIGHER** YOU WILL TEND TO HIT THE BALL

SO, YOU AUTOMATICALLY START TO SWING **FLAT** IN ORDER TO KEEP THE BALL DOWN

IF YOU SPEND MORE THAN ABOUT 4 OR 5 DAYS PLAYING IN WINDY WEATHER YOU ARE BOUND TO GET YOUR SWING A LITTLE BIT FLAT

WHEN THIS HAPPENS, PRACTISE SWINGING CLOSE TO A WALL, A FENCE OR A TREE – ANYTHING WHICH WILL FORCE YOU TO SWING **UPRIGHT**. DO THIS UNTIL YOUR SWING IS ONCE AGAIN IN ITS **PROPER** GROOVE.

77

Don't tee the ball too low

THIS WILL ACTUALLY CAUSE YOU TO HIT THE BALL TOO HIGH BECAUSE YOU WILL TEND TO SWING TOO STEEPLY IN AN EFFORT TO GET THE BALL AIRBORNE

YOU WILL **CHOP DOWN** ON THE THING LIKE AN IRON-SHOT AND PUT **BACKSPIN** ON THE BALL WHICH WILL MAKE IT **CLIMB**

YOU MUST TRY TO GET A MUCH **SHALLOWER** ANGLE OF ATTACK, AND THE WAY TO DO THIS, IS TO TEE THE BALL **HIGH**. THEN YOU WILL BE ABLE TO DRIVE THE BALL **FORWARD**

MOST PEOPLE THINK THAT THEY HAVE TO TRY TO KEEP THE BALL DOWN WHEN HITTING INTO THE WIND. THIS IS NOT SO. WHAT YOU MUST TRY TO DO IS TO MAKE A **GOOD, CONVINCING HIT,** THEN THE BALL WILL AUTOMATICALLY KEEP GOING THROUGH THE WIND

87

My four key thoughts

FIRSTLY, I THINK OF PLACING THE CLUBHEAD **SQUARE** BEHIND THE BALL

THEN I CHECK THAT MY FEET ARE LINED UP SQUARE TO THE TARGET

THIRDLY, I THINK ABOUT MY HANDS AND MAKE SURE THAT THEY ARE SET **SLIGHTLY AHEAD** OF THE BALL

FINALLY, I MOVE MY HEAD A LITTLE BIT **BACK TO THE RIGHT**

DURING THE ACTUAL GOLFSWING, THERE IS ONLY TIME TO THINK OF **ONE** THING. NORMALLY, I THINK OF KEEPING MY HEAD **BEHIND** THE BALL UNTIL I HAVE HIT IT

50

When you drive too high

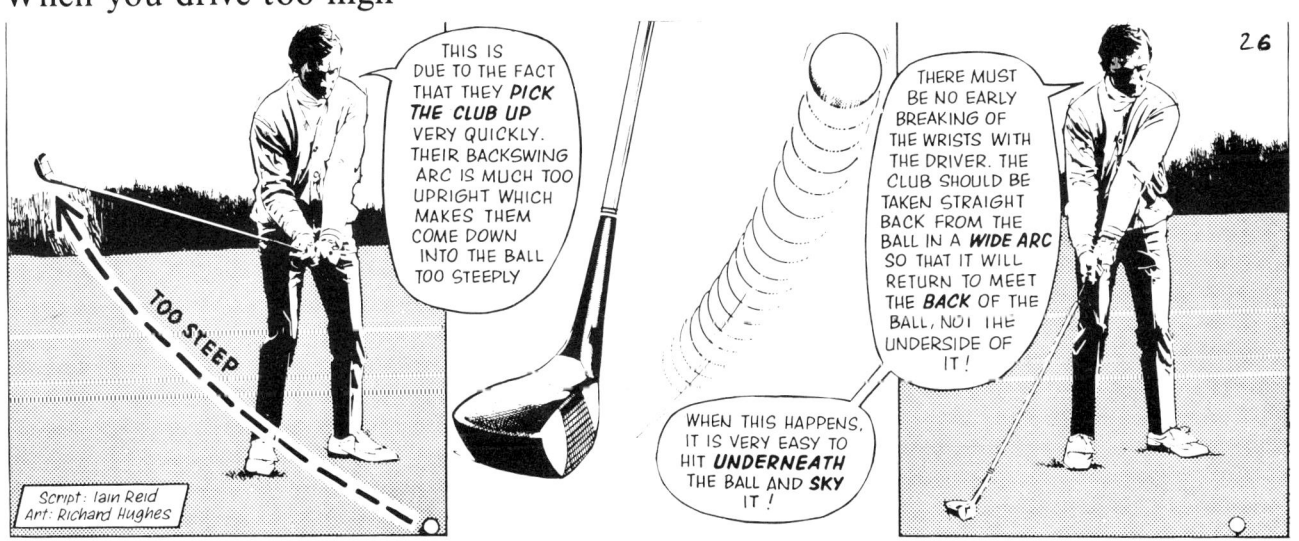

THIS IS DUE TO THE FACT THAT THEY **PICK THE CLUB UP** VERY QUICKLY. THEIR BACKSWING ARC IS MUCH TOO UPRIGHT WHICH MAKES THEM COME DOWN INTO THE BALL TOO STEEPLY

TOO STEEP

THERE MUST BE NO EARLY BREAKING OF THE WRISTS WITH THE DRIVER. THE CLUB SHOULD BE TAKEN STRAIGHT BACK FROM THE BALL IN A **WIDE ARC** SO THAT IT WILL RETURN TO MEET THE **BACK** OF THE BALL, NOT THE UNDERSIDE OF IT!

WHEN THIS HAPPENS, IT IS VERY EASY TO HIT **UNDERNEATH** THE BALL AND **SKY** IT!

26

Script: Iain Reid
Art: Richard Hughes

When a golfer sways

Slowing your rhythm

I had trouble with my grip

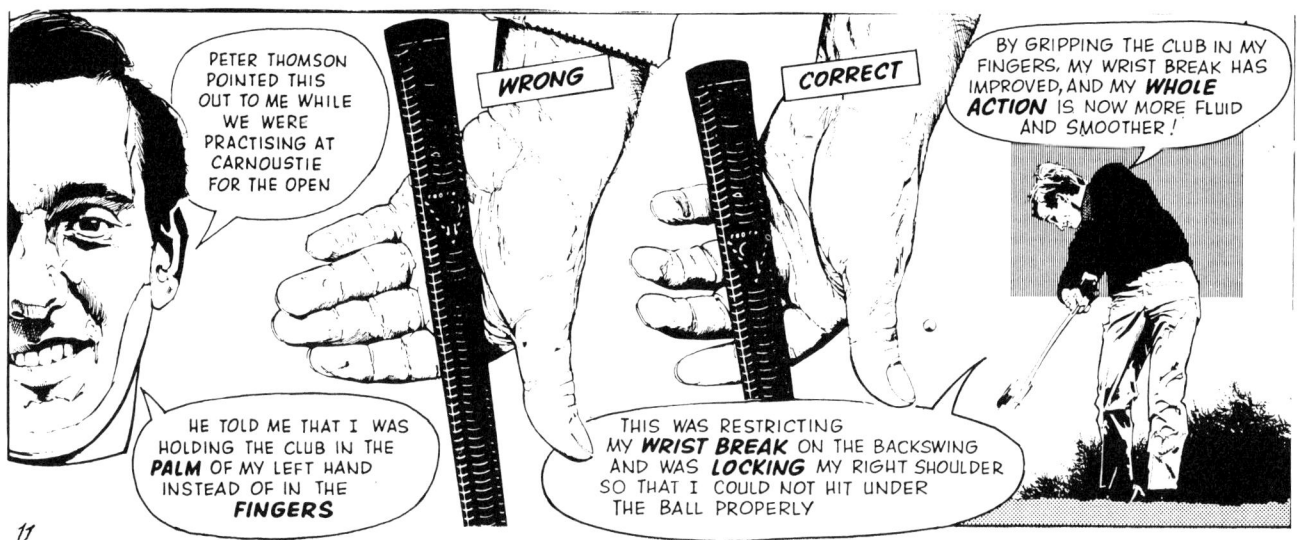

I couldn't aim straight

I was much too wristy

Playing off mats

Teaching youngsters in America

The head must be still.

Most beginners reach for their drivers at every opportunity, because they know it is the club that will give them most distance. What they fail to realise is that it is also the hardest club to control.

The margin of error increases steeply as the loft of the clubface decreases – and the driver has virtually no loft at all.

So, if you are going to be able to handle this vital club properly, you must first learn the mechanics and techniques that apply specifically to the drive.

This chapter will show you how to set-up properly, swing smoothly and finish with a high, relaxed follow through. It will also point out some of the common mistakes even the best golfers make, and suggest ways to overcome them.

The drive

My swing was very flat

I STARTED TO HIT SNAP HOOKS AND PUSHES! I COULDN'T UNDERSTAND WHAT WAS WRONG UNTIL IT WAS POINTED OUT TO ME THAT MY SWING HAD BECOME *VERY FLAT!*

THE ONE-PIECE TAKEAWAY

I THEN CHECKED MY TAKEAWAY AND DISCOVERED THAT, WHEN I REACHED *THIS* POSITION, MY WRISTS WERE BECOMING *LOCKED* — I HAD NO WRIST BREAK AT ALL. THIS WAS FORCING MY ARMS TO TRAVEL *FLAT* AROUND MY BODY

HAVING TRACED THE FAULT, I KNEW WHAT TO DO TO CORRECT IT. WHEN MY HANDS REACHED THIS POSITION, I CONCENTRATED ON BREAKING MY WRISTS AND MAKING MY ARMS TRAVEL *UPWARDS* AS STEEPLY AS POSSIBLE

THIS UPRIGHT SWING ELIMINATED MY *QUICK HOOKS* AND *BIG PUSHES!*

Script: Iain Reid
Art: Richard Hughes

I kept hitting far right

I WAS TAKING THE CLUB BACK FROM THE BALL NICE AND LOW BUT I WAS GETTING INTO A SLIGHTLY *FLAT* POSITION AT THE TOP WITH MY CLUB POINTING *LEFT* OF THE TARGET

THEN, WHEN I CAME BACK DOWN INTO THE BALL, I WAS ARRIVING A LITTLE BIT AHEAD WITH THE CLUBFACE OPEN! THE BALL WOULD START OFF TO THE RIGHT, THEN FADE A LITTLE BIT MORE TO THE RIGHT!

OPEN

I NOW CONCENTRATE ON MAKING MY SWING SLIGHTLY MORE *UPRIGHT.* THE CLUB POINTS MORE TOWARDS THE TARGET AND THE CLUBFACE IS A LITTLE MORE OPEN AT THE TOP OF THE SWING

THIS MAKES ME ARRIVE BACK INTO THE BALL IN A *SQUARE* POSITION WHICH PRODUCES A STRAIGHT SHOT. THIS TWO OR THREE INCH DIFFERENCE IN POSITION AT THE TOP OF THE SWING MAKES UP TO *50 YARDS* DIFFERENCE IN THE SHOT

SQUARE

49

I was leading a tournament but playing poorly

... BUT I WAS A LITTLE UNHAPPY ABOUT THE WAY I KEPT **BLOCKING** THE BALL IN THE THIRD ROUND— I WAS NOT GETTING MY RIGHT HAND INTO THE SHOT ! SO, OVER LUNCH, I ASKED NORMAN VON NIDA'S ADVICE

WELL, PETER, IT'S NO GOOD THINKING ABOUT YOUR **HANDS !** IT'S FAR BETTER TO THINK ABOUT GETTING YOUR RIGHT LEG TO PASS YOUR LEFT LEG, AND STAYING BEHIND THE BALL

BEFORE LUNCH

AFTER LUNCH

I WENT OUT AND HIT A FEW PRACTICE SHOTS AND DISCOVERED THAT NORMAN WAS ABSOLUTELY RIGHT !

AS LONG AS I STAYED BEHIND THE BALL AND MADE AN EFFORT TO GET MY RIGHT LEG PAST MY LEFT, I HAD NO FEAR OF BLOCKING THE BALL AND LEAVING IT OUT TO THE RIGHT

3

Using the legs properly

WHEN YOU SWING TOO FAST, YOUR HANDS GET AHEAD OF THE BALL AND AHEAD OF YOUR **LEG** ACTION. THEREFORE, THE CLUBHEAD HITS THE BALL FAR TOO **LATE** AND SENDS IT STRAIGHT OUT TO THE RIGHT

NORMAN VON NIDA GAVE ME A VERY USEFUL TIP. HE TOLD ME TO CONCENTRATE ON GETTING THE CORRECT **LEG ACTION** AND NOT TO THINK OF MY **HANDS !**

HE TOLD ME TO THINK ONLY OF MOVING MY LEFT LEG BACK AND MY RIGHT LEG THROUGH—NOTHING ELSE ! BY DOING THIS, I FOUND THAT MY HANDS WORKED **WITH** MY LEGS INSTEAD OF INDEPENDENTLY— AND MY WHOLE SWING SLOWED DOWN IMMEDIATELY !

22

Peter Townsend is a superb iron player. His power and accuracy with the long and medium clubs has always been a feature of his play, but he also has a sure touch around the greens.

In this chapter, he explains the differing characteristics of the iron clubs and how to choose the correct one for a specific golfing situation.

Many beginners are mystified by the distances the pros are able to achieve with certain clubs, when they themselves can rely only on certain " favourites " to see them safely home.

Learning to match the club to the situation is what this chapter is all about – plus judgement of distance and understanding how differing lies can affect the shape and length of a shot, often by as much as 20 or 30 yards.

Iron play

My hands were behind at address

The importance of tempo

Cutting down hand action

I changed my set-up

My left arm sometimes lets me down

The arms should work together

Move the head to the right

Nicklaus said my hands were way behind

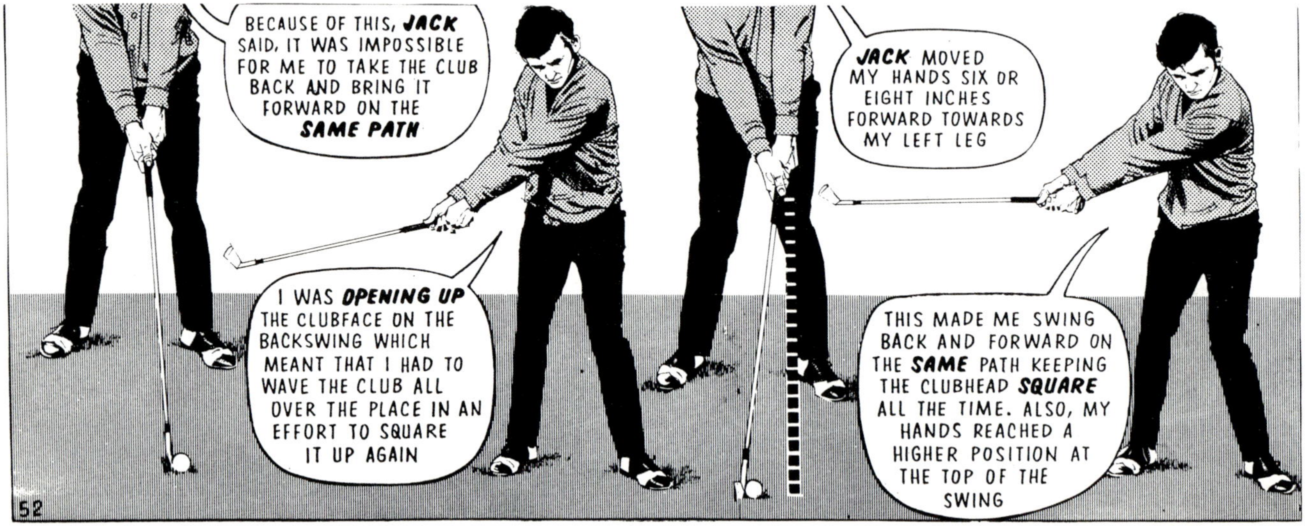

I came off the ball

THIS WAS DUE TO MY INCORRECT ADDRESS POSITION. I WAS **BENDING** MY HEAD AND SHOULDERS TO THE BALL INSTEAD OF **STANDING TALL.** CONSEQUENTLY, I WAS BOUND TO **JUMP UP** ON THE SHOT!

STRAIGHT LEGS

SOUTH AFRICAN GOLFER, COBIE LEGRANGE, GAVE ME A VERY GOOD TIP THAT HELPED ME SET MYSELF UP **TALL.** HE TOLD ME TO STAND **COMPLETELY UPRIGHT** IN A NATURAL MANNER

I FIND THAT, BY STANDING TALL TO THE BALL, MY SWING ARC IS **MUCH WIDER** AND I HIT THROUGH THE BALL WITH MY ARMS **EXTENDED** INSTEAD OF CRAMPED!

THEN, ALL I HAD TO DO TO GET INTO THE PERFECT ADDRESS POSITION WAS TO **FLEX MY KNEES!**

LEGS BENT

The fairway woods (2, 3 and 4) are among the most versatile weapons in the golfer's bag. Many beginners have difficulty controlling long irons and turn to the wooden clubs in a kind of desperation.

To their surprise, they find that they can not only cope with them easily but achieve considerable distance at the same time.

The extra loft on the wooden clubs and the wider hitting area is what makes them that much easier to handle and their use is by no means confined to the fairway.

As Peter Townsend explains, a club as versatile as the 4-wood can be used off the tee, in the rough, even out of a bunker. Once you have mastered the technique, those long par - 5 holes suddenly become less intimidating.

Fairway woods

My head was drooping

THIS TENSION BUILD-UP PREVENTED MY SHOULDERS FROM TRAVELLING BACK AND FORWARD *UNDERNEATH* MY CHIN

THIS CREATED A LOT OF *TENSION* IN THE TOP HALF OF MY BODY

WRONG

THEN MY SHOULDERS WERE FREE TO WORK AS THEY SHOULD DO

I CORRECTED THIS BY HOLDING MY HEAD OUT UNTIL I WAS IN A RELAXED, COMFORTABLE POSITION

RIGHT

64

At the Ryder Cup I couldn't stop fading

OVER LUNCH, I ASKED *JOHN JACOBS* THE REASON FOR THIS AND HE SAID THAT I HAD THE BALL POSITIONED *TOO FAR BACK* IN MY STANCE

THIS MEANT THAT, WHEN I CAME INTO THE BALL, I WAS NOT QUITE IN THE CORRECT POSITION TO HIT. MY CLUBFACE WAS MAKING CONTACT BEFORE IT WAS *SQUARED* UP TO THE HOLE. HENCE THE FADE!

JOHN SUGGESTED THAT I MOVE THE BALL FORWARD *THREE INCHES*, WHICH I DID

THESE THREE INCHES GAVE ME *MORE TIME* TO CLEAR MY LEFT SIDE OUT OF THE WAY OF MY HANDS AND, CONSEQUENTLY, MORE *FREEDOM* TO HIT THROUGH THE BALL

Arthur Lees helped me a lot

I thought I'd got it right

With his vast experience on golf courses all over the world, Peter Townsend can claim to have faced pretty nearly every golfing situation at some time or another.

Playing around trees, through trees, over trees, from the side of a hill or the top... these hazards are all in a day's work to the professional golfer.

The average player, however, sees it rather differently. And in showing how to cope with such situations, Townsend also demonstrates how you can make the correct decisions when faced with a choice of playing safely – or gambling everything.

The over-riding lesson is that more strokes are wasted through lack of thought and concentration than through lack of skilled play.

On the course

I try and hit straight in a breeze

BUT, AT THE END OF LAST YEAR, I WAS HITTING EVERYTHING *STRAIGHT TO THE RIGHT!* THE TROUBLE STEMMED FROM ADDRESSING THE BALL *TOO FAR BACK* IN MY STANCE — A HABIT THAT HAD CREPT IN WITHOUT MY NOTICING!

CONSEQUENTLY, WHEN I MOVED *SLIGHTLY FORWARD* COMING INTO THE BALL, I WAS THEN *TOO FAR AHEAD* AND NOT IN A POSITION TO TAKE MY HANDS THROUGH TO THE TARGET. THEY WERE GOING TO THE *RIGHT* — AND I WAS HITTING THE BALL AT THE WRONG *ANGLE OF ATTACK*

I POSITIONED THE BALL A LITTLE FURTHER FORWARD SO THAT, WHEN I MOVED ON TO THE BALL, IT WAS *STILL* AHEAD OF ME!

I WAS THEN ABLE TO CLEAR MY LEFT SIDE AND HIT THE BALL STRAIGHT!

Check your right arm at address

How I regain confidence

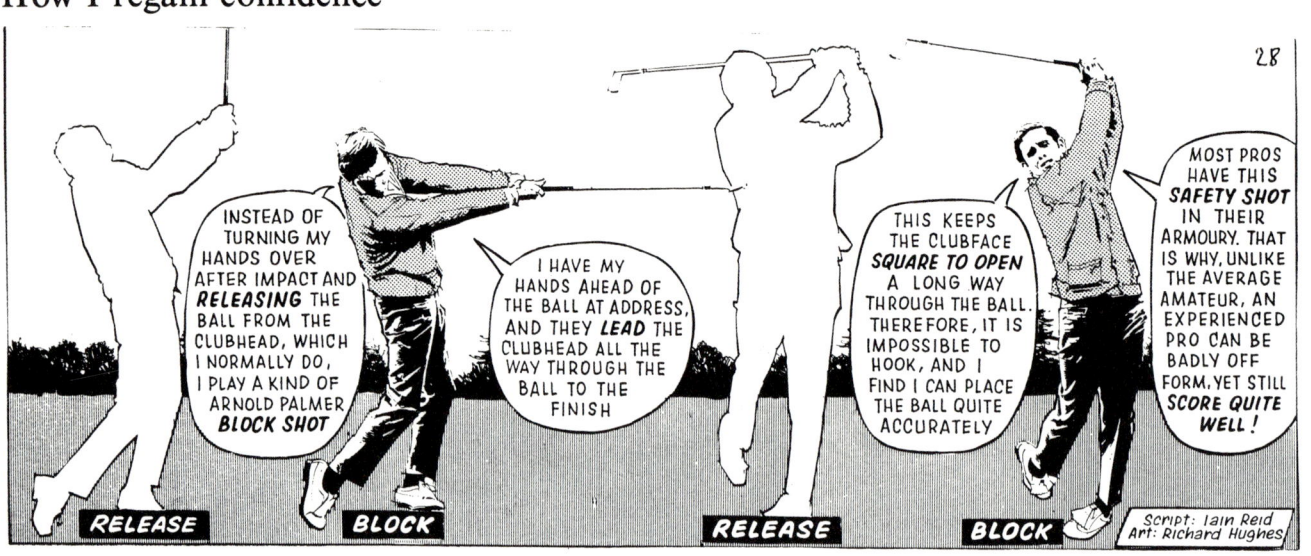

A sure cure for hooking

Dai Rees gave me good advice

ON A PAR THREE HOLE, DAI WATCHED ME **THROW** THE BALL DOWN ON TO THE TEEING AREA AND HIT MY SHOT

HE TOLD ME ALWAYS TO **TEE** THE BALL UP WHENEVER THE RULES PERMITTED

WHEN YOU TEE THE BALL UP, IT IS MUCH EASIER TO GET THE **BACKSPIN** YOU NEED TO KEEP THE SHOT UNDER CONTROL

AND, WHEN PLAYING **DOWNWIND**, WHERE THE WIND IS ALWAYS TRYING TO PUSH THE BALL DOWN, IT IS NOT POSSIBLE TO TEE THE BALL **TOO HIGH**. TEE THE BALL WELL UP, SO THAT YOU CAN GET THE CLUBHEAD GOING THROUGH UNDERNEATH IT

John Jacobs spotted a serious fault

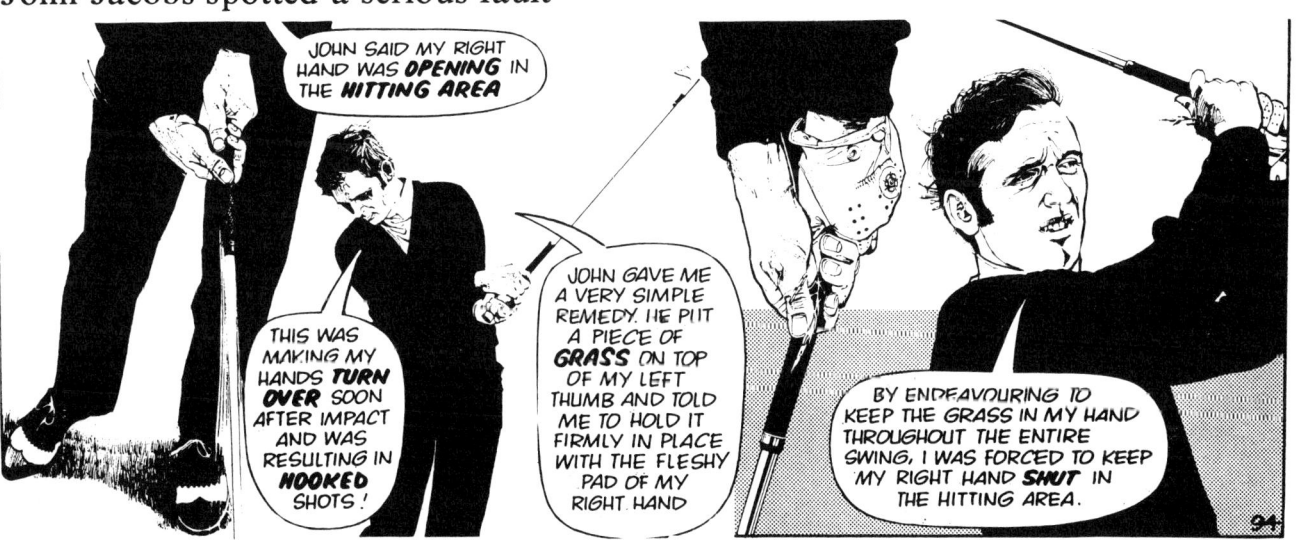

JOHN SAID MY RIGHT HAND WAS **OPENING** IN THE **HITTING AREA**

THIS WAS MAKING MY HANDS **TURN OVER** SOON AFTER IMPACT AND WAS RESULTING IN **HOOKED** SHOTS!

JOHN GAVE ME A VERY SIMPLE REMEDY. HE PUT A PIECE OF **GRASS** ON TOP OF MY LEFT THUMB AND TOLD ME TO HOLD IT FIRMLY IN PLACE WITH THE FLESHY PAD OF MY RIGHT HAND

BY ENDEAVOURING TO KEEP THE GRASS IN MY HAND THROUGHOUT THE ENTIRE SWING, I WAS FORCED TO KEEP MY RIGHT HAND **SHUT** IN THE HITTING AREA.

It is the ability to save shots around
the green that separates the good golfer from the average.
Touch, finesse, accuracy, judgement of distance...
these are the qualities required, and they are the hardest
to achieve without practice.

In this chapter, Peter Townsend explains how to choose
the correct club for a specific situation; how to impart backspin;
how to stop the ball quickly, or make it run on.

If you are a reliable pitcher and chipper –
an expert at rolling three shots into two – you will
win a lot more matches than you ever lose.

Around the green

Take care in a crosswind

WHEN PITCHING IN A RIGHT TO LEFT WIND, I MOVE THE BALL A LITTLE BIT MORE TOWARDS MY LEFT FOOT INSTEAD OF PLAYING IT OFF MY RIGHT FOOT

THIS ENABLES ME TO CLEAR MY SIDE QUICKER AND TO SWING IN A PATH WHERE I COME **SLIGHTLY ACROSS** THE BALL. THIS IS A TYPE OF **FADE** SHOT

WHEN THE WIND IS BLOWING FROM LEFT TO RIGHT, I POSITION THE BALL BACK TOWARDS MY **RIGHT** FOOT

THIS GIVES ME AN IN-TO-OUT ACTION, AND I **HOOK** THE BALL WHICH HELPS IT TO HOLD ITS COURSE DESPITE THE WIND

When it's wise to play short

HERE I AM HITTING TO A **FAST** GREEN THAT SLOPES DOWN TOWARDS ME. MY PLAN IS TO KNOCK IT **CLOSE** TO THE FLAG BUT NOT **PAST** IT AS I DO NOT WANT A **FAST, DOWNHILL** PUTT!

SIMILARLY, WHEN THE GREEN IS **FAST** AND IT SLOPES **AWAY** FROM ME, I TRY TO GET MY BALL PAST THE HOLE TO LEAVE MYSELF AN **UPHILL** PUTT!

HOWEVER, THIS DOES NOT APPLY ON **VERY SLOW** GREENS. AN UPHILL PUTT ON A SLOW GREEN IS **MUCH HARDER** THAN A DOWNHILL PUTT

Run-up shots are easiest

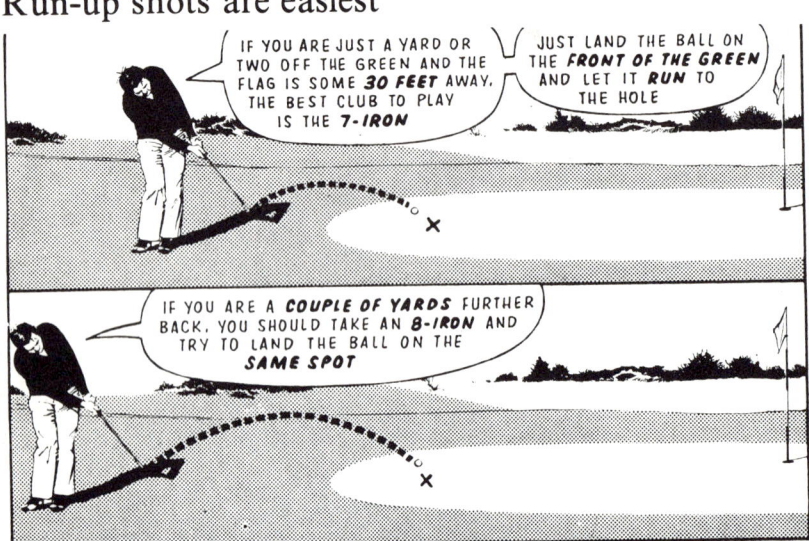

69

The secret of wedge play

92

50

The Americans are deadly at pitch and run

Californian pros have a unique chipping method

The putting green is the one part of golf
where the professional and the amateur can meet on equal terms.
Or that's what the amateur deludes himself into thinking.
Because while it's true that anyone of us is capable of sinking
a 10 foot putt, few of us are capable of doing it consistently.

The professional, says Peter Townsend, strives
to eliminate luck as much as it's possible to do so, by building
a consistent striking method and learning to read and understand
even the most subtly contoured of greens.

The secret, of course, is practice and in this chapter
Townsend suggests some practice drills which can make you
a better putter, and explains too how to set yourself up to give
yourself the best possible chance of holing out.

Putting

Good putters are relaxed putters

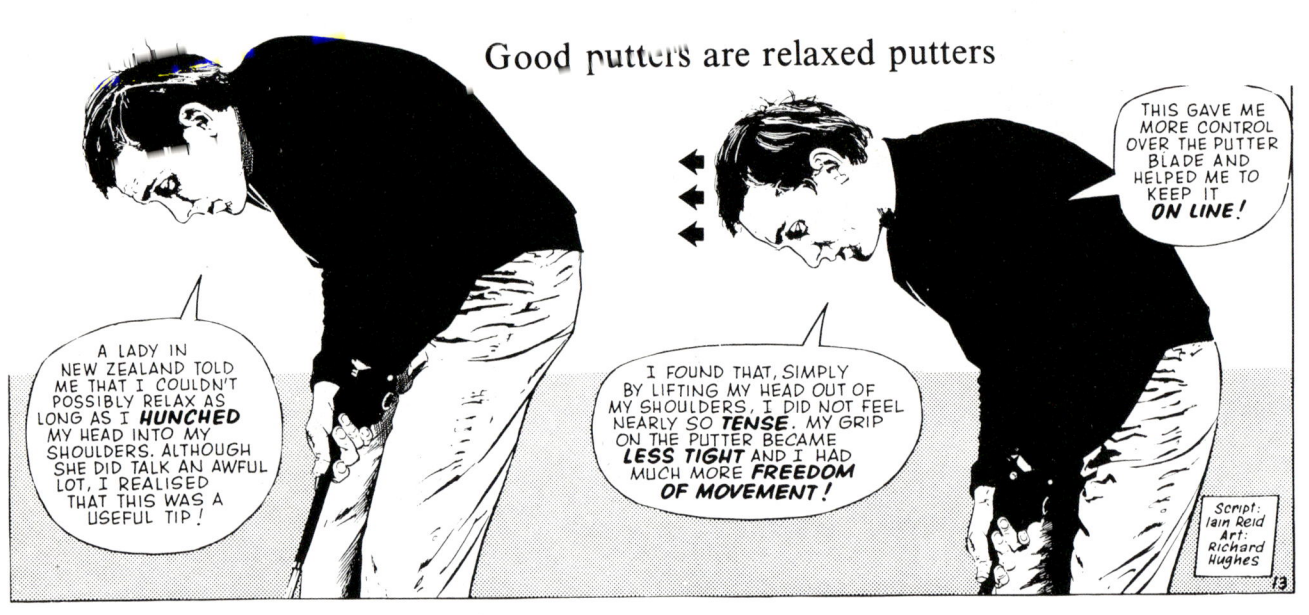

I sometimes get too far from the ball

54

How to stop dragging putts

I couldn't keep the putterhead going through

Move the clubhead straight through

Setting the blade square

Rain makes a difference

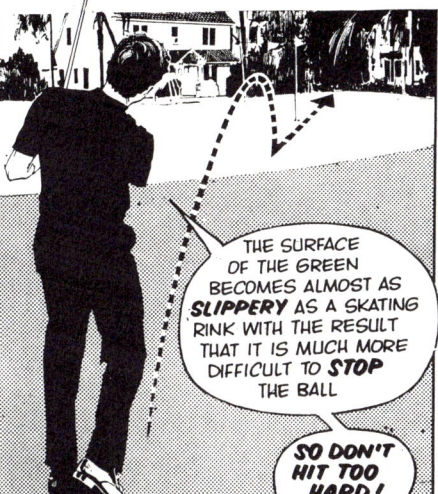

THE SURFACE OF THE GREEN BECOMES ALMOST AS *SLIPPERY* AS A SKATING RINK WITH THE RESULT THAT IT IS MUCH MORE DIFFICULT TO *STOP* THE BALL

SO DON'T HIT TOO HARD!

NOW, WHEN IT COMES TO *PUTTING* ON A RECENTLY WET GREEN, DON'T MAKE THE MISTAKE OF FEELING YOU HAVE TO *BELT* THE BALL TO GET IT UP TO THE HOLE

IN MY EXPERIENCE, A SLIGHT SHOWER HARDLY AFFECTS THE PACE OF THE GREEN. IT MIGHT MAKE IT A *SHADE* SLOWER – BUT THAT IS ALL!

82

My hands were working independently

83

I FELT AS IF MY LEFT HAND WAS *BREAKING QUICKLY* AWAY FROM THE BALL, AND THAT MY RIGHT HAND WAS *OVERTAKING* ON THE FORWARD SWING

THIS HAS HELPED A GREAT DEAL AND MY HANDS NOW WORK IN HARMONY AS A SINGLE UNIT

I DECIDED TO TRY PUTTING WITH MY HANDS *LOCKED* TOGETHER USING THE GRIP WHICH *JACK NICKLAUS* ADOPTS FOR *ALL* HIS SHOTS

BAD

INTERLOCK

Putting in strong winds

I couldn't handle bumpy greens

How to read greens

I USE THE **PLUMB LINE** METHOD QUITE FREQUENTLY, BUT **NEVER** WHEN IT IS VERY **WINDY!** THE PUTTER GETS BLOWN ABOUT TOO MUCH TO GIVE **FOOLPROOF** RESULTS!

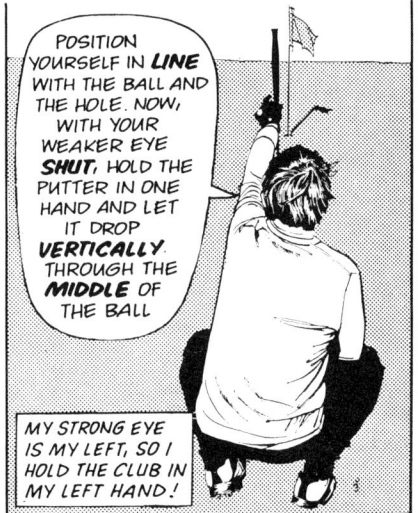

POSITION YOURSELF IN **LINE** WITH THE BALL AND THE HOLE. NOW, WITH YOUR WEAKER EYE **SHUT**, HOLD THE PUTTER IN ONE HAND AND LET IT DROP **VERTICALLY** THROUGH THE **MIDDLE** OF THE BALL

MY STRONG EYE IS MY LEFT, SO I HOLD THE CLUB IN MY LEFT HAND!

IF THE HOLE APPEARS ON THE **RIGHT** OF THE CLUB, THE BALL WILL BREAK FROM **LEFT TO RIGHT**—AND VICE VERSA

IF THE HOLE APPEARS IN **LINE** WITH THE CLUB, IT IS A **STRAIGHT PUTT**

99

Use your imagination

ONCE I AM STANDING OVER THE BALL, I SLOWLY LIFT MY HEAD AND TRY TO FOLLOW THE **LINE** THE BALL IS GOING TO TAKE TO THE HOLE

I TRY TO **IMAGINE** THE BALL TAKING THE VARIOUS **BORROWS** THAT I CAN SEE BETWEEN IT AND THE HOLE

BY THE TIME I COME TO STRIKE THE BALL, I HAVE A **MENTAL PICTURE** OF THE **PATH** THE BALL WILL TAKE AND, THIS IS IMPORTANT, I CAN "**SEE**" THE BALL GOING INTO THE HOLE!

I FIND THAT THIS METHOD KEEPS ME FROM GETTING **JUMPY**, AND HELPS ME TO MAKE A NICE, **SMOOTH STROKE!**

100

A useful putting tip

Tony Jacklin set me thinking

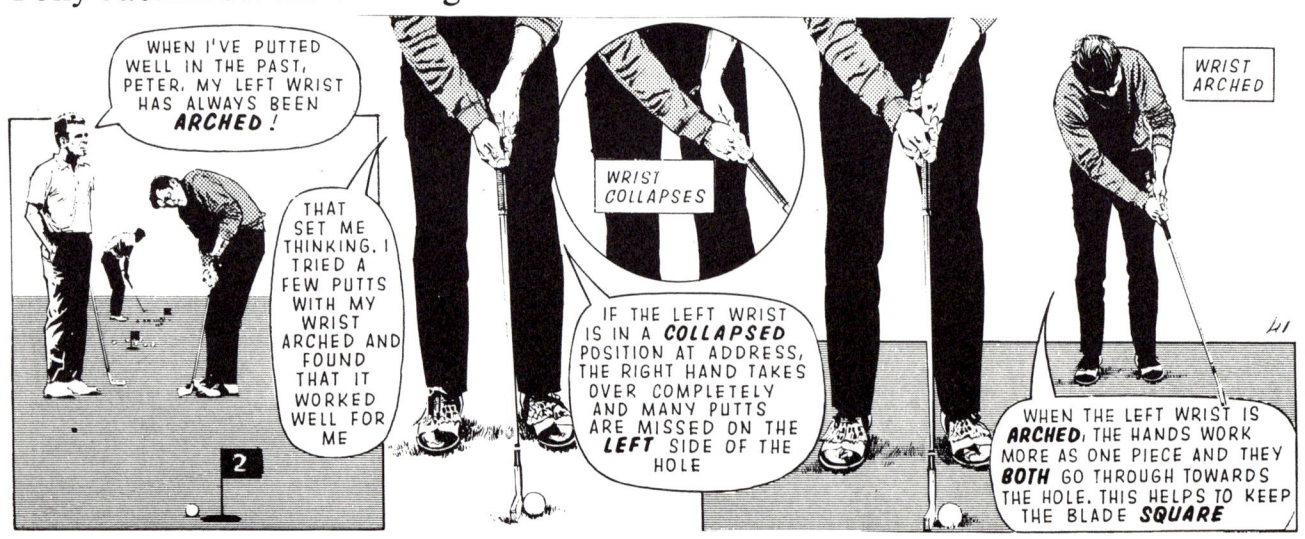

A good practice tip

WHEN YOU ARE PRACTISING BEFORE GOING OUT TO PLAY, TRY PUTTING FROM ABOUT FIVE FEET, STRIKING THE BALL WITH THE *TOE* OF THE CLUB

YOU WILL HAVE TO TAKE THE PUTTER BACK *VERY SLOWLY* AND *SQUARELY* TO HAVE ANY CHANCE OF HITTING THE BALL IN THE RIGHT DIRECTION

PERSEVERE WITH THIS FOR TEN MINUTES THEN RETURN TO THE NORMAL WAY OF PUTTING

YOU WILL FIND THAT YOU HAVE A MUCH BETTER AND *MORE CONSISTENT STROKE* AND THAT EVERYTHING SEEMS TO COME RIGHT OFF THE *MIDDLE* OF THE BLADE — A MARVELLOUS FEELING!

53

Max Faulkner spotted a flaw

84

ACCORDING TO *MAX*, I WAS MISSING A LOT OF *SHORT PUTTS* BECAUSE MY BACKSWING WAS TOO LONG, AND THE CLUBHEAD WAS *SLOWING DOWN* AS IT CAME INTO THE BALL

SHORTEN YOUR BACKSWING AND *LENGTHEN* YOUR FOLLOW-THROUGH

I TOOK MAX'S ADVICE AND NOW MY CLUBHEAD *ACCELERATES* THROUGH THE BALL, AND I AM CONSCIOUS OF GIVING IT A MUCH MORE *POSITIVE* HIT!

Most golfers faced with a bad lie in thick rough
will simply take a deep breath and then expend every ounce
of muscle in an attempt to hack the ball clear.

Usually, the result is deeper rough and greater effort.
Trouble shots such as these can be overcome once the golfer
becomes aware of the proper procedures and abandons pure strength
in favour of planned strategy and a controlled swing.

You won't escape trouble on the golf course –
even the Jack Nicklaus', of this world have their fair
share of it – but you can avoid a ruinous score.

Trouble shots

No divot if it's wet

EITHER YOU WILL "FLY" THE BALL, AND HAVE NO CONTROL OVER THE **LENGTH** OF THE SHOT, OR YOU WILL HIT IT **VERY HEAVY**

IN WET WEATHER, YOU SHOULD POSITION THE BALL **SLIGHTLY FURTHER FORWARD**. THIS WILL HELP YOU TO HIT THE BALL **CLEANLY**— THAT IS, ON THE UPSWING RATHER THAN ON THE DOWNSWING

HOWEVER, WHEN YOU MOVE THE BALL FORWARD IN YOUR STANCE, IT IS IMPORTANT TO MOVE YOUR **HANDS** FORWARD ALSO, OTHERWISE YOU WILL TEND TO HIT **BEHIND** THE BALL!

ON WET, SOGGY TURF, I ALSO **REDUCE** THE WIDTH OF MY STANCE SLIGHTLY, WHICH PREVENTS ME FROM SLIPPING ALL OVER THE PLACE!

ANGLE OF ATTACK

ANGLE OF ATTACK

Script: Iain Reid
Art: Richard Hughes

Playing irons off a downslope

I ADDRESS THE BALL CLOSER TO MY **LEFT** FOOT THAN I WOULD DO ON **LEVEL** GROUND

I TRY TO **CUT** THE SHOT SLIGHTLY TO GET THE BALL UP IN THE AIR WITHOUT HAVING TO **FORCE** IT

I LET MY WEIGHT **MOVE FORWARD** FREELY SO THAT I AM ALMOST **WALKING** AFTER THE SHOT THE MOMENT I HIT IT

BAD

ON THIS PARTICULAR TYPE OF SLOPE, THE AVERAGE PLAYER MAKES THE MISTAKE OF LEAVING HIS WEIGHT **BEHIND**, WHICH IS NO GOOD AT ALL!

10B

Swing slowly in heavy rough

HANDS IN FRONT

BLADE OPEN

BUT FIRST, IT IS IMPORTANT TO ASSUME THE CORRECT SET-UP POSITION WITH THE HANDS *SLIGHTLY AHEAD* OF THE BALL AND THE BLADE A LITTLE BIT *OPEN*

I BREAK MY WRISTS FAIRLY QUICKLY ON THE BACKSWING. THIS IS ONE SHOT WHERE A LONG, LOW BACKSWING IS NOT CALLED FOR

I COME INTO THE BALL AND CONTINUE THROUGH TO THE FINISH AT AN EASY, *UNIFORM* PACE

THERE MUST BE NOTHING JERKY ABOUT THIS SHOT, EVEN THOUGH THE LIE MAY NOT BE VERY GOOD. I DON'T SO MUCH *HIT* THE BALL OUT OF THE ROUGH AS *SWEEP* IT OUT!

SWEEP

42

Getting long irons airborne

47

When the hands should take over

Adjust your club for a good lie

66

When the ball is above you

88

> IF YOU ADDRESS IT IN THE NORMAL, *RELAXED* POSITION, YOU WILL VERY LIKELY HIT THE THING 'FAT' OR 'HEAVY'!

> *PAUL HAHN*, THE FAMOUS TRICK SHOT ARTIST FACES THE SAME KIND OF SHOT WHEN HE PLAYS THE BALL OFF A *THREE FOOT* HIGH TEE

> PAUL GAVE ME HIS SECRET. YOU MUST STAND AS *FAR AWAY* FROM THE BALL AS YOU CAN WITHOUT BEING *COMPLETELY* UNCOMFORTABLE. STRETCH OUT YOUR ARMS

> FROM THIS POSITION, YOU SHOULD BE ABLE TO HIT THE BALL CLEANLY

Royal Birkdale taught me a lesson

TROUBLE

> PLAYING THERE IN THE *RYDER CUP* MATCHES I WORKED OUT A PLAN WHICH WAS A GREAT HELP TO ME

> IF THE TROUBLE WAS ON THE *RIGHT* OF THE GREEN, I SET MYSELF UP ON THE LEFT AND AIMED TO *FADE* THE BALL ON TO THE FLAG

> IF THE TROUBLE WAS ON THE LEFT, I AIMED TO THE RIGHT, AND PLAYED THE SHOT WITH *DRAW*

> BY DOING THIS, I FELT I WAS KEEPING OUT OF THE WAY OF THE TROUBLE – NOT HITTING DIRECTLY TOWARDS IT. CONSEQUENTLY, I DID NOT BECOME OBSESSED BY THE TROUBLE, WHICH IS FATAL WHEN YOU HAVE TO HIT A *3-WOOD* SOME *250 YARDS* TO A GREEN

58

The average golfer approaches a bunker with the same
relish as he might approach a pit of snakes.
Bunkers mean dropped shots, ruined scores and nightmares.

It needn't be so. There is nothing particularly sinister about
sand and indeed, putting the ball close to the hole from a bunker
is usually a far simpler task than fighting clear of heavy rough.

Like most things in golf, it's really a question
of confidence – confidence built on a sound technique
and experience of varying conditions.

Gary Player, the world's greatest exponent of
the bunker shot, frequently holes out from the greenside sand trap.
Suggest he has been lucky and he will answer quite simply,
"The more I practise, the luckier I get!"

That in essence is the secret of practice.

Playing a wood from a bunker

OBVIOUSLY, YOU MUST HAVE A **GOOD LIE**, AND THE TRAP MUST NOT HAVE A BIG **"LIP"**

GRIP THE CLUB SHORT

YOU MUST ENDEAVOUR TO MAKE A **VERY SLOW** TAKEAWAY FROM THE BALL. DON'T JERK AT ALL BECAUSE YOUR **BALANCE** IS NEVER ALL THAT GOOD IN SAND

SWING AS **SLOWLY** AS YOU CAN AND KEEP YOUR SWING AS **SHORT** AS POSSIBLE TO CUT OUT UNNECESSARY **BODY MOVEMENTS** THAT MIGHT UPSET YOUR BALANCE

SHORT

KEEP YOUR HEAD **VERY STILL** AND HIT THROUGH **SMOOTHLY!**

SLOW

BALL OPPOSITE LEFT FOOT

6B

Gary Player helped me improve

GARY PLAYER ASKED ME WHAT I CONCENTRATED ON WHEN PLAYING BUNKER SHOTS. I REPLIED THAT I JUST LOOKED AT THE BALL AND TRIED TO GET IT OUT

GARY SAID THAT WAS THE **WORST** THING I COULD DO! HE SAID I MUST **NEVER** LOOK AT THE BALL IN A BUNKER—I MUST PICK A SPOT BEHIND THE BALL AND LOOK AT THAT!

NORMAN VON NIDA ALSO GAVE ME A GOOD PIECE OF ADVICE. WHEN YOUR BALL IS **PLUGGED** IN A BUNKER, IT IS IMPOSSIBLE TO GET BACKSPIN, SO PLAY IT WITH THE CLUBFACE **CLOSED** RATHER THAN OPEN. THIS MAKES IT EASIER TO CONTROL THE **RUN** OF THE BALL!

OPEN

CLOSED

NORMAL LIE

PLUGGED LIE

14

If you have difficulties in the sand

IT COULD BE THAT THE **LIE** OF YOUR **SAND WEDGE** IS NOT RIGHT FOR YOU!

IF, FOR EXAMPLE, YOUR CLUB HAS TOO **FLAT** A LIE, THE **TOE** WILL DIG IN DEEPER THAN THE **HEEL**. IT IS VERY HARD TO HIT **CONSISTENT** SHOTS IF YOU ARE TAKING **MORE SAND** AT ONE END OF THE CLUBHEAD THAN AT THE OTHER!

IT IS A SIMPLE JOB TO CHECK YOUR CLUB'S LIE. HAVE A SWING IN SOFTISH SAND THEN LOOK TO SEE IF THE DIVOT IS **DEEPER** AT ONE END

IF IT IS, TELL YOUR PRO, AND HE WILL ALTER THE LIE OF THE CLUB TO SUIT YOU!

DIVOT DEEPER HERE

A thump shot can help a plugged lie

Don't look at the ball, look behind it

Don't try and dig yourself out

The speed of shot can vary

If the ground slopes away

When the sand is wet

Two different approaches

It is not sufficient simply to master the basic skills of golf. The player who scores consistently well does so because he is also able to think his way around the course, saving shots through prudence and a planned strategy.

For the average player, that means knowing when to select a three wood instead of a driver on a particularly tight hole; taking two putts instead of three by examining the green carefully before he plays; taking a short iron from a fairway bunker instead of going for distance with a longer club; and aiming for the side of the fairway that offers least trouble should the shot be mis-hit.

Golf is a game that requires planned thought and patience. So, to achieve a good score you must take each hole as it comes, assess the problems, and make each shot accordingly.

Don't fight the wind

Overcoming first tee nerves

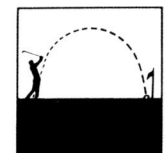

Don't let blind holes make you anxious

IF YOU HAVE TO DRIVE OVER A HILL AND YOU KNOW THERE IS TROUBLE AT THE OTHER SIDE OF IT, THE CHANCES ARE YOU WILL *LOOK UP* QUICKLY AND RUIN THE SHOT

WHAT YOU OUGHT TO DO IS FORGET ALL ABOUT THE TREES OR THE BUNKERS WAITING TO CLAIM YOUR BALL, AND CONCENTRATE ON AIMING AT THE GUIDE POST ON TOP OF THE HILL

DECIDE THAT YOU ARE GOING TO TAKE A REALLY *GOOD SWING* AT THE BALL AND THAT YOU ARE TO STAY DOWN ON THE SHOT. IN OTHER WORDS MAKE UP YOUR MIND TO WATCH THE BALL *BEFORE* YOU HIT IT, NOT *AFTER!*

Hooking into a left-right wind

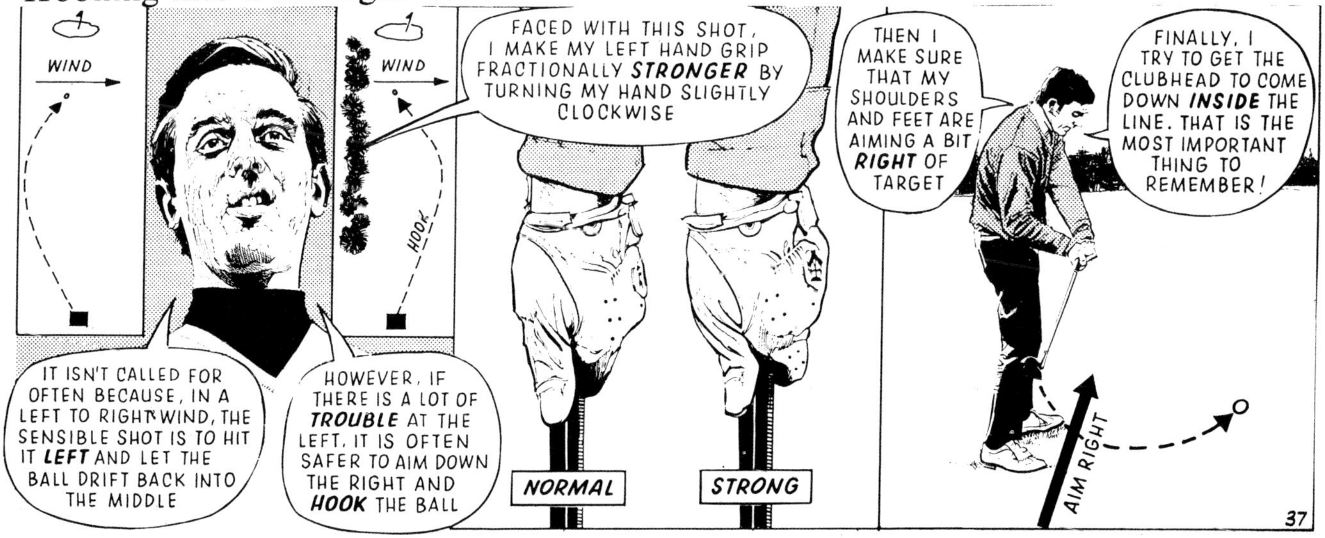

WIND

WIND

HOOK

IT ISN'T CALLED FOR OFTEN BECAUSE, IN A LEFT TO RIGHT WIND, THE SENSIBLE SHOT IS TO HIT IT *LEFT* AND LET THE BALL DRIFT BACK INTO THE MIDDLE

HOWEVER, IF THERE IS A LOT OF *TROUBLE* AT THE LEFT, IT IS OFTEN SAFER TO AIM DOWN THE RIGHT AND *HOOK* THE BALL

FACED WITH THIS SHOT, I MAKE MY LEFT HAND GRIP FRACTIONALLY *STRONGER* BY TURNING MY HAND SLIGHTLY CLOCKWISE

NORMAL

STRONG

THEN I MAKE SURE THAT MY SHOULDERS AND FEET ARE AIMING A BIT *RIGHT* OF TARGET

FINALLY, I TRY TO GET THE CLUBHEAD TO COME DOWN *INSIDE* THE LINE. THAT IS THE MOST IMPORTANT THING TO REMEMBER!

AIM RIGHT

37

If you habitually hook, check your left wrist

If there's danger, stay down longer

Mannerisms can help you relax

When you should underclub

A good lie doesn't always help

Why club golfers mess up golf's easiest shot

Be firm and positive in choosing clubs

Take account of all trouble areas

84

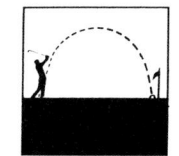

I could almost reach the par-5's in two

HOWEVER, THE FAIRWAY GRASS WAS A BIT **LONG** AND THE FLAGS WERE ON THE **FRONT** OF THE GREENS GUARDED BY BIG BUNKERS

IT WAS VERY HARD TO CLEAR THE BUNKER AND **STOP** THE BALL QUICKLY ENOUGH

I DECIDED THAT IT WAS MUCH EASIER TO STOP AN **80-YARD** SAND WEDGE SHOT THAN A 20-YARD ONE

3-WOOD

DRIVER

SO, INSTEAD OF HITTING, SAY A DRIVER AND A 3-WOOD, I WOULD HIT A DRIVER AND A 3-IRON AND LEAVE MYSELF A **FULL SAND WEDGE** SHOT TO THE GREEN

3-IRON

DRIVER

THEN I WAS ABLE TO GET ENOUGH **ACTION** ON THE BALL TO STOP IT REASONABLY CLOSE TO THE HOLE

85

Bob Murphy has good first tee psychology

HE HITS HIS LAST FEW BALLS ON THE PRACTICE GROUND WITH HIS **DRIVER**, HITTING THE TYPE OF SHOT HE INTENDS TO PLAY OFF THE **FIRST TEE!**

FOR EXAMPLE, IF THE FIRST HOLE HAS A BIG BUNKER ON THE RIGHT WHICH MAKES IT ADVISABLE TO HIT DOWN THE LEFT SIDE WITH A BIT OF A HOOK, BOB HITS A FEW **PRACTICE HOOKS!**

HOLE NUMBER ONE

HOOK

IF, ON THE OTHER HAND, THERE IS **OUT OF BOUNDS** ON THE **LEFT** AND BOB WANTS TO **FADE** THE BALL DOWN THE RIGHT HAND SIDE, HE PRACTISES A FEW FADE SHOTS LIKE THIS BEFORE LEAVING THE PRACTICE AREA

36

Henry Cotton is such a positive thinker

WE WERE TALKING ABOUT DRIVING WHEN YOU ARE **UNDER PRESSURE**. FOR EXAMPLE, WHEN YOU NEED TO SHOOT A **PAR FOUR** AT THE **18th** TO WIN THE TOURNAMENT— AND IT'S **OUT OF BOUNDS** ON THE LEFT !

HENRY SAID THAT, WHENEVER IT WAS **IMPERATIVE** THAT HE SHOULD HIT THE FAIRWAY, HE USED TO TRY TO PICTURE HIMSELF **FINISHING** THE SWING IN **EXHIBITION STYLE !**

HE DIDN'T WORRY ABOUT THE REST OF THE SWING. ALL HE WAS CONCERNED ABOUT WAS GETTING INTO A **PERFECTLY BALANCED POSITION** AT THE END.

My recipe for a perfect swing !

THE IDEAL GOLFSWING IS PROBABLY AN IMPOSSIBILITY, BUT HERE ARE THE QUALITIES I WOULD LIKE TO POSSESS . . .

CLUB POINTS TO TARGET
HANDS HIGH

LEFT HAND HAS NOT TURNED OVER

33

NO EARLY WRIST BREAK

FANTASTIC KNEE ACTION

LONG EXTENSION — AN ABSOLUTE MUST

GARY PLAYER'S ADDRESS AND TAKEAWAY

TOM WEISKOPF'S POSITION AT THE TOP OF THE SWING

NICKLAUS'S ABILITY TO ATTACK THE BALL FROM THE **INSIDE**

PALMER'S GREAT EXTENSION THROUGH THE BALL

BERT YANCEY'S PERFECTLY-BALANCED FINISH !

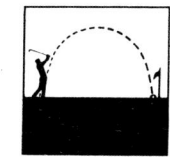

Roberto de Vincenzo helped me aim left safely

I THOUGHT A LOT ABOUT THIS, AND NOW IT IS A *BIG THING* WITH ME. I CONCENTRATE HARD ON TAKING MY LEFT HAND THROUGH TO THE HOLE AND *FINISHING HIGH!*

GOOD

BAD

THIS USED TO BE *SUICIDE* BECAUSE OF MY TENDENCY TO *HOOK!* MY HANDS USED TO *ROLL OVER* AND FINISH UP ROUND MY BACK!

ROBERTO TOLD ME THAT HIS MAIN THOUGHT DURING THE SWING IS TO FINISH WITH HIS *HANDS HIGH* SO THAT HIS LEFT HAND DOES NOT TURN OVER. THIS CUTS OUT HOOKING COMPLETELY!

Script: Iain Reid
Art: Richard Hughes

Glossary

Some Guidance to the Rules of Golf

Since the Game of Golf is not played in a small defined area with a single moving ball, the Rules are necessarily more complicated than in most other games. The Golf Foundation have, therefore, prepared the following summary of some of the basic Rules with which the new player should be familiar in even his earliest rounds. It is stressed that only the briefest outline is given.

And while this summary has the whole-hearted approval of the Rules of Golf Committee of the Royal and Ancient Golf Club, it cannot be applied in settling any dispute which may arise in play; for that purpose the text of the official Rules must always be referred to.

This summary is accordingly in no sense a substitute for the Rules themselves, which every player should study. In particular, the attention of players entering for competitions or matches is drawn to Rules 36 and 37.

Ball played as it lies

You must play the ball as it lies, unless the Rules allow you to do otherwise.

Improving lie prohibited

You must not press down anything which would improve your lie; but outside a hazard you may remove loose impediments such as leaves, loose branches and twigs, wormcasts, provided that the ball does not move during or after their removal.

You may not improve your line of play, your lie or the area of your intended swing, by moving, breaking or bending anything growing except in fairly taking your stance or in making your stroke.

Wrong ball

There are penalties for playing someone else's ball (except in a hazard), so put a mark on your ball to help you identify it.

Ball at rest moved

If you move your ball accidentally, you must play it as it lies under penalty of one stroke.

Ball lost, out of bounds or unplayable

If you cannot find your ball after looking for it for five minutes, if you abandon it as lost, with or without searching for it, or if you hit it out of bounds, you must play your next stroke from where you played the original stroke, counting that stroke and adding a penalty stroke to your score (this penalty is known as "stroke and distance").

If you hit your ball into what you consider to be an unplayable lie, you may drop the ball, adding one penalty stroke, either within two club-lengths of the unplayable spot, but not nearer the hole, or anywhere directly behind it; alternatively, you may play another stroke, as in the previous paragraph, with penalty of stroke and distance.

Provisional ball

If you think that your ball may be lost or out of bounds, to save time you may play a provisional ball from the original spot before going forward, and you may go on playing this ball until you reach the place where the original ball is likely to be.

If then you find your original ball in bounds and playable, you must pick up the provisional one: if the original ball is lost or out of bounds, you may continue with the provisional ball with the penalty of stroke and distance as in the first paragraph of the previous section.

If, however, your original ball is in bounds, but unplayable, you may not continue with the provisional ball, but proceed with either of the alternatives in the second paragraph of the previous section, i.e. dropping under penalty of one stroke or going back to the original spot with stroke and distance penalty.

Obstructions

An obstruction is something artificial erected or placed on the Course but does not include fences and walls marking out of bounds.

If the obstruction interferes with your play and is moveable you may move it.

If it is immovable, and if it interferes with your stance or intended swing, then you may drop your ball two club-lengths from the point on the outside of the obstruction nearest which it lay, but not nearer the hole, without penalty.

Casual water, ground under repair, hole made by a burrowing animal

Casual water is any temporary accumulation of water. Ground under repair is any part of the Course so marked, and includes material such as grass mowings piled for removal, even if not so marked.

If your ball lies or is lost in, or your stance or swing is interfered with by casual water, ground under repair or a hole made by a burrowing animal, you may drop the ball two club-lengths away from the affected area, but not nearer the hole, without penalty.

If this situation arises when your ball is in a hazard, then you may drop in the hazard without penalty, or behind the hazard under penalty of one stroke.

If your ball is on the green, and these conditions interfere, or intervene between your ball and the hole, you may place the ball on the nearest spot avoiding these conditions, not nearer the hole.

Hazards and water hazards

When your ball is in a bunker or a water hazard, you may not, before making a stroke, touch the ground or water with your club in addressing the ball or in any other way, nor may you test the condition of the bunker, except that you may take up a firm stance.

You may not touch or move a loose impediment in a hazard.

When your ball is anywhere in a water hazard, you may drop it as far behind the hazard as you wish, keeping the spot where it entered the hazard between yourself and the hole, under penalty of one stroke, or you may play another stroke from where you played the original stroke under penalty of stroke and distance.

When your ball is in a lateral water hazard, which means that it is impossible to drop behind as above, then you may drop within two club-lengths on either side under penalty of one stroke.

The flagstick

You may always have the flagstick attended, removed, or held up to indicate the position of the hole, but you must decide on this before you play your stroke ; the flagstick is entirely under your control.

If your ball strikes the flagstick, when attended, or, if played from the putting green strikes it when attended or unattended, you lose the hole in match play and suffer a penalty of two strokes in medal play.

The putting green

You may clean your ball on the green.

You may repair pitch-marks on the green.

If your opponent's ball interferes with your play, you may ask him to lift it.

If in match play your ball strikes your opponent's ball, he may replace it or play it from where it lies at his option, and you suffer no penalty: but if in medal play both balls are on the putting green, there is a two stroke penalty for striking the other ball, which must be replaced.

You may not play the ball on the green with a stance astride the line of your putt in the manner of a croquet player.

Undue delay

You must at all times play without undue delay.

Etiquette

Holes in Bunkers:
Before leaving a bunker, a player should carefully fill up and smooth over all holes and footprints made by him.

Restore Divots and Ball-Marks:
Through the Green, a player should ensure that any turf cut or displaced by him is replaced at once and pressed down, and that any damage to the putting green made by the ball or the player is carefully repaired.

Damage to Greens—Flagsticks, Bags etc.:
Players should ensure that, when putting down bags, or the flagstick no damage is done to the putting green, and that neither they nor their caddies damage the hole by standing close to it, in handling
the flagstick or in removing the ball from the hole. The flagstick should be properly replaced in the hole before the players leave the putting green.

Golf Carts:
Local notices regulating the movements of golf carts should be strictly observed.

Damage through Practice Swings:
In taking practice swings players should avoid causing damage to the course, particularly the tees, by removing divots.